21st Century Hits

Six Chord Songbook

Wise Publications
part of The Music Sales Group
London/New York/Sydney/Paris/Copenhagen/Berlin/Madrid/Tokyo

The *Six Chord Songbook* allows even the beginner guitarist to play and enjoy the best rock and pop tunes. With the same 6 chords used throughout the book, you'll soon master playing your favourite hits.

The *Six Chord Songbook* doesn't use music notation. Throughout the book chord boxes are printed at the head of each song; the chord changes are shown above the lyrics. It's left up to you, the guitarist, to decide on a strum rhythm or picking pattern.

You might find the pitch of the vocal line is not always comfortable because it is pitched too high or two low. In that case, you can change the key without learning a new set of chords; simply place a capo behind a suitable fret.

Whatever you do, this *Six Chord Songbook* guarantees hours of enjoyment for guitarists of all levels, as well as providing a fine basis for building a strong repertoire.

Published by:
Wise Publications,
8/9 Frith Street, London W1D 3JB, England.

Exclusive Distributors:
Music Sales Limited,
Distribution Centre, Newmarket Road,
Bury St. Edmunds, Suffolk IP33 3YB, England.
Music Sales Pty Limited,
120 Rothschild Avenue, Rosebery, NSW 2018, Australia.

Order No.AM84740
ISBN 0-7119-2646-8
This book © Copyright 2003 by Wise Publications.

Compiled by Lucy Holliday.
Arranged by James Dean.
Music processed by Paul Ewers Music Design.
Photographs courtesy of London Features International.
Printed in the United Kingdom by
Caligraving Limited, Thetford, Norfolk.

Your Guarantee of Quality
As publishers, we strive to produce every book
to the highest commercial standards.
The music has been freshly engraved and the book
has been carefully designed to minimise awkward page
turns and to make playing from it a real pleasure.
Particular care has been given to specifying acid-free,
neutral-sized paper made from pulps which have not
been elemental chlorine bleached. This pulp is
from farmed sustainable forests and was
produced with special regard for the environment.
Throughout, the printing and binding have been
planned to ensure a sturdy, attractive publication
which should give years of enjoyment.
If your copy fails to meet our high standards,
please inform us and we will gladly replace it.

www.musicsales.com

Relative Tuning

The guitar can be tuned with the aid of pitch pipes or dedicated electronic guitar tuners which are available through your local music dealer. If you do not have a tuning device, you can use relative tuning. Estimate the pitch of the 6th string as near as possible to E or at least a comfortable pitch (not too high, as you might break other strings in tuning up). Then, while checking the various positions on the diagram, place a finger from your left hand on the:

5th fret of the E or 6th string and **tune the open A** (or 5th string) to the note (A)

5th fret of the A or 5th string and **tune the open D** (or 4th string) to the note (D)

5th fret of the D or 4th string and **tune the open G** (or 3rd string) to the note (G)

4th fret of the G or 3rd string and **tune the open B** (or 2nd string) to the note (B)

5th fret of the B or 2nd string and **tune the open E** (or 1st string) to the note (E)

E	A	D	G	B	E
or	or	or	or	or	or
6th	5th	4th	3rd	2nd	1st

Head

Nut

1st Fret

2nd Fret

3rd Fret

4th Fret

5th Fret

Reading Chord Boxes

Chord boxes are diagrams of the guitar neck viewed head upwards, face on as illustrated. The top horizontal line is the nut, unless a higher fret number is indicated, the others are the frets.

The vertical lines are the strings, starting from E (or 6th) on the left to E (or 1st) on the right.

The black dots indicate where to place your fingers.

Strings marked with an O are played open, not fretted.
Strings marked with an X should not be played.

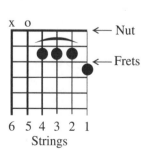

The curved bracket indicates a 'barre' - hold down the strings under the bracket with your first finger, using your other fingers to fret the remaining notes.

All The Things She Said

Words & Music by
Sergei Galoyan, Trevor Horn, Martin Kierszenbaum,
Elena Kiper & Valerij Polienko

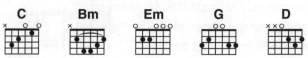

Capo first fret

Intro ‖: C | Bm | Em | G :‖ N.C. |

Chorus 1
C
All the things she said,
    Bm
All the things she said,
        Em
Running through my head,

Running through my head,
G
Running through my head.
C
All the things she said,
    Bm
All the things she said,
       Em
Running through my head,

Running through my head,
G
All the things she said.
C   **Bm Em**   **G**
This is not enough.

Interlude | C | Bm | Em | G |

Verse 1
     Em
I'm in serious s***,

I feel totally lost.
    D
If I'm asking for help,

It's only because,

G
Being with you has opened my eyes,

    Bm
Could I ever believe such a perfect surprise?

      Em
I keep asking myself,

Wondering how.

    D
I keep closing my eyes,

But I can't block you out.

    G
Wanna fly to a place,

Where it's just you and me.

Bm
Nobody else, so we can be free,

(Nobody else, so we can be free).

Chorus 2   As Chorus 1

C   **Bm Em**   **G**
This is not enough (all the things she said),

(All the things she said).

Instrumental ‖: **Em** | **Em** | **D** | **D** | **G** | **G** | **Bm** | **Bm** :‖

            C
Verse 2   And I'm all mixed up,

      Bm
Feeling cornered and rushed.

      Em
They say it's my fault,

cont.

        D
But I want her so much.

        C
Wanna fly her away,

        Bm
Where the sun and the rain,

        Em
Come in over my face,

        D
Wash away all the shame.

        C
When they stop and stare,

        Bm
Don't worry me,

        Em
'Cause I'm feeling for her,

        D
What she's feeling for me.

        C
I can try to pretend,

        Bm
I can try to forget,

        Em
But it's driving me mad,

Going out of my (head).

Chorus 3   As Chorus 1

C   **Bm** **Em**   **G**
This is not enough (all the things she said),

(All the things she said).
C   **Bm**
  All the things she said, all the things she said.
Em   **G**
All the things she said, all the things she said.
                  C
All the things she said, all the things she said.
Bm   **Em**
  She said,   all the things she said.
G
All the things she said.

(C)   (Bm)
Mother looking at me

(Em)   (G)
Tell me what do you see?

(C) (Bm)   (Em)
Yes I lost my mind.

(C)   (Bm)
Daddy looking at me,

(Em) (G)
Will I ever be free,

(C)   (Bm)   (Em)
Have I crossed the line?

Chorus 4

C
All the things she said,

      Bm
All the things she said,

            Em
Running through my head,

Running through my head,

G
Running through my head.

C
All the things she said,

      Bm
All the things she said,

            Em
Running through my head,

Running through my head,

G
All the things she said.

C   Bm Em   G
This is not enough.

C   Bm Em   G
This is not enough.

N.C.
All the things she said, all the things she said,

All the things she said, all the things she said,

All the things she said.

Big Sur

Words by Conor Deasy
Music by Conor Deasy, Kevin Horan, Pádraic McMahon, Daniel Ryan & Ben Carrigan
Contains elements from "Theme From The Monkees" -
Words & Music by Tommy Boyce & Bobby Hart

Am   G   Bm   C   Em   D

Intro | Am | G | Am | Bm   ‖

Verse 1
    C   **Em**
   So much for the city
Am
Tell me that you'll dance to the end,
    C   **D   Em**
Just tell me that you'll dance to the end.
    C   **Em**
   Hey, hey you're the Monkees,
     Am
The people said you monkeyed around,
    C   **D   Em**
But nobody's listening now.

Chorus 1
    G   **C**   **Am**   **D**
   Just don't go back to Big Sur,
Am   **C**
   Hangin' a - round,
Am   **C**
   Lettin' your old man down
G   **C**   **Am**
   Just don't go back to Big Sur,
D   **C**
Baby, baby, please don't go.
   D   **G   Bm**
Oh, baby, baby, please don't go.

Verse 2
```
        C                Em
     So much for the street lights,
            Am
     They're never gonna guide you home,
           C                              D   Em
     No, they're never gonna guide you home.
        C                Em
        Down at the steamboat show, yeah,
        Am
     All the kids start spitting
                        C            D   Bm
     I guess I didn't live up to the billing.
```

Chorus 2
```
     G          C        Am      D
        Just don't go back to Big Sur,
     Bm         C
        Hangin' a - round,
     Bm                       C
        Lettin' your old man down
     G          C        Am
        Just don't go back to Big Sur,
     D                        C
     Baby, baby, please don't go.
           D                  G       Bm
     Oh, baby, baby, please don't go.
```

Instrumental | Am | G | Am | G   Bm ‖

               | C | Em | Em | Em |

               | C | C D | Em | Em   ‖

Chorus 3   As Chorus 2

9

Born To Try

Words & Music by
Delta Goodrem & Audius Mtawarira

G	D	Em	Am

Intro | G |

Verse 1

G   D   Em
Doing everything that I believe in,

G   D   Em
Going by the rules that I've been taught.

G   D   Em
More understanding of what's around me,

G   D   Em
And protected from the walls of love.

Am   G   D
All that   you see is me,

Am   G   D
And all I truly believe.

Chorus 1

                 G
That I was born to try,

D   Em
I've learned to love.

          G
Be understanding,

D   Em
And believe in life.

                Am
But you've got to make choices,

G   D
Be wrong or right,

               Am   G   D
Sometimes you've got to sacrifice the things you like.

                G
But I was born to try.

Verse 2

G   D   Em
No point in talking what should   have been,

G   D   Em
In regretting the things that went on.

G   D   Em
Life's full of mistakes, destinies and fate,

G   D   Em
Remove the clouds look at the bigger picture now.

Am   G   D
And all that   you see is me,

Am   G   D
And all I truly believe.

Chorus 2

                  G
That I was born to try,

D   Em
I've learned to love.

        G
Be understanding,

D   Em
And believe in life.

                Am
But you've got to make choices,

G   D
Be wrong or right,

             Am   G   D
Sometimes you've got to sacrifice the things you like.

            G
But I was born to try.

Middle

‖: Am   G   D
   All that   you see is me,

Am   G   D
And all I truly believe. :‖

Chorus 3

                  G
That I was born to try,

D   Em
I've learned to love.

        G
Be understanding,

D   Em
And believe in life.

                Am
But you've got to make choices,

cont.

    G   **D**
    Be wrong or right,

                    Am   **G**   **D**
Sometimes you've got to sacrifice the things you like.

          (G)
But I was born to try.

‖: **G**   **D** | **Em**   :‖

                   Am
But you've got to make choices,

G   **D**
   Be wrong or right.

                    Am   **G**   **D**
Sometimes you've got to sacrifice the things you like.

N.C.   **(G)**
But I was born to try.

Complicated

Words & Music by
Avril Lavigne, Lauren Christy, Scott Spock & Graham Edwards

Intro

Em C
    Uh huh,
G D
 Life's like this.
Em   C   G   D | Em C
 Uh huh,   uh huh, that's the way it is.
G   D
 'Cause life's like this,
Em   C   G   D
 Uh huh, uh huh that's the way it is.

Verse 1

G
 Chill out whatcha yellin' for?
Em
 Lay back, it's all been done before,
C   D
 And if you could only let it be you will see.
G
 I like you the way you are,
Em
 When we're drivin' in your car,
C   D
 And you're talking to me, one on one but you've become,

Bridge 1

       C
Somebody else round everyone else,

          Em
You're watching your back like you can't relax.

        C   D
You're tryin' to be cool, you look like a fool to me.

Tell me,

Chorus 1

Em   C   G
Why'd you have to go and make things so complicated?
 D
I see the way you're
Em   C   G
Acting like you're somebody else gets me frustrated
D
Life's like this you,
Em   C
   And you fall and you crawl and you break,
       G   D
And you take what you get and you turn it into
Am   C
Honesty and promise me, I'm never gonna find you fake it,
       G
No, no, no.

Verse 2

G
   You come over unannounced,
Em
   Dressed up like you're somethin' else,
C   D
   Where you are and where it's at you see,

You're making me
G
   Laugh out when you strike your pose,
Em
   Take off all your preppy clothes,
C   D
   You know you're not fooling anyone,

When you've become

14

Bridge 2   As Bridge 1

Chorus 2   As Chorus 1

Interlude | (G) | Em | C | D   ‖

Verse 3
```
G
```
       Chill out whatcha yelling for?
```
Em
```
       Lay back, it's all been done before,
```
C                         D
```
       And if you could only let it be, you will see

Bridge 3   As Bridge 1

Chorus 3
```
       Em                        C              G
```
       Why'd you have to go and make things so complicated?
```
          D
```
       I see the way you're
```
       Em                        C              G
```
       Acting like you're somebody else gets me frustrated
```
       D
```
       Life's like this you,
```
       Em                        C
```
       And you fall and you crawl and you break,
```
             G                         D
```
       And you take what you get and you turn it into
```
       Am                                        C
```
       Honesty and promise me, I'm never gonna find you fake it, no, no

Chorus 4
```
       Em                        C              G
```
       Why'd you have to go and make things so complicated?
```
          D               Em                    C
```
       I see the way you're acting like you're somebody else
```
             G       D
```
       Gets me frustrated. Life's like this you,
```
       Em                        C
```
       And you fall and you crawl and you break,
```
             G                         D
```
       And you take what you get and you turn it into
```
       Am                                        C
```
       Honesty and promise me, I'm never gonna find you fake it, no, no, no.

15

Danger! High Voltage

Words & Music by
Tyler Spencer, Joseph Frezza, Stephen Narawa & Anthony Selph

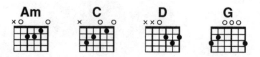

Intro | Am | Am | Am | Am | Am | Am |

Verse 1

Am   C
Fire in the disco,

D   Am   D G
Fire in the taco bill.

Am   C
Fire in the disco,

D   Am   D G
Fire in the gates of hell.

Verse 2

Am   C
Don't you wanna know how we keep starting fires?

D   Am   D   G
It's my desire, it's my desire, it's my desire.

Am   C
Don't you wanna know how we keep starting fires?

                  D
It's my desire, it's my desire,

Am   D G
It's my desire.

Chorus 1

Am   C
Danger, danger!   High voltage,

D   Am   D G
When we touch,   when we kiss.

Am   C
Danger, danger!   High voltage,

D   Am   D   G
When we touch, when we kiss, when we touch.

Chorus 2

Am   C
Danger, danger!   High voltage,

D   Am   D G
  When we touch,   when we kiss.

Am   C
Danger, danger!   High voltage,

D   Am
  When we touch, when we kiss,

        D   G
When we touch, when we (kiss).

Guitar Solo ‖: Am | C | D | Am D G :‖ *x4*
   kiss.

Verse 3

       Am   C
Well don't you wanna know how we keep starting fires?

D   Am   D G
  It's my desire,   it's my desire.

Am   C
Don't you wanna know how we keep starting fires?

D   Am   D G
  It's my desire,   it's my desire.

Chorus 3   As Chorus 1

Chorus 4   As Chorus 1

Sax Solo ‖: Am | C | D | Am D G :‖

Verse 4

Am
Fire in the disco,

C
Fire in the disco,

D   Am   D G
Fire in the taco bill.

Am
Fire in the disco,

C
Fire in the disco,

D   Am   D G
Fire in the gates of hell.

Outro | Am | C | D | Am D G |
                The gates of hell.

  ‖: Am | C | D | Am D G :‖
                                  Repeat to fade

Fight Test

Words & Music by
Wayne Coyne, Steven Drozd, Michael Ivans, David Fridman & Cat Stevens

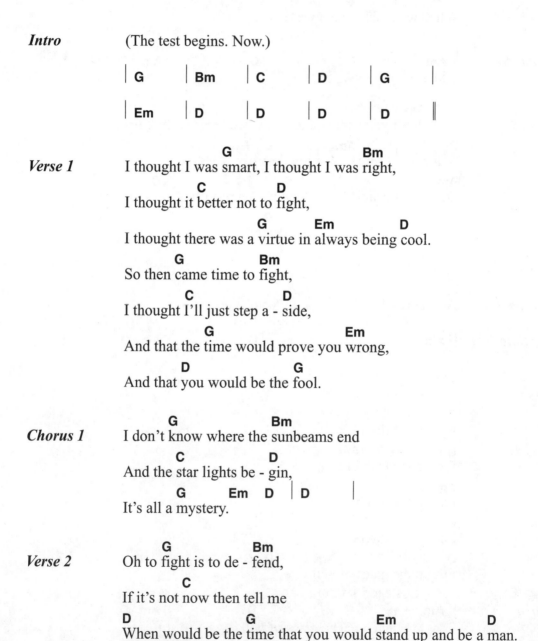

Intro

(The test begins. Now.)

| G | Bm | C | D | G |
| Em | D | D | D | D |

Verse 1

               G   Bm
I thought I was smart, I thought I was right,
       C   D
I thought it better not to fight,
                   G   Em   D
I thought there was a virtue in always being cool.
           G   Bm
So then came time to fight,
        C   D
I thought I'll just step a - side,
             G   Em
And that the time would prove you wrong,
        D   G
And that you would be the fool.

Chorus 1

            G   Bm
I don't know where the sunbeams end
        C   D
And the star lights be - gin,
        G   Em D | D |
It's all a mystery.

Verse 2

           G   Bm
Oh to fight is to de - fend,
         C
If it's not now then tell me
D   G   Em   D
When would be the time that you would stand up and be a man.

                G   Em
For to lose I could ac - cept,

                      C   D
But to sur - render I just wept

                              G   Em
And regretted this moment

                    D
Oh that I,

                  G   Bm
I don't know where the sunbeams end

                    C   D
And the star lights be - gin,

                  G   Em   D
It's all a mystery.

                      G   Bm
And I don't know how a man decides

                    C   D
What's right for his own life,

                  G   Em   D | D
It's all a mystery.

                  G   Bm
'Cause I'm a man, not a boy,

                    C   D
And there are things you can't a - void,

                  G
You have to face them,

                  Em   D
When you're not prepared to face them.

                G   Em
If I could I would,

                        C
But you're with him now,

                  D
It do no good,

                    G
I should have fought him

                Em   D
But in - stead I let him,

                  G
I let him take you.

Chorus 3

         G   **Bm**
I don't know where the sunbeams end
        C   **D**
And the star lights be - gin,
        G   **Em** **D**
It's all a mystery.
           G   **Bm**
And I don't know how a man decides
      C   **D**
What's right for his own life,
        G   **Em** **D**
It's all a mystery.

Bridge | **C** | **C** | **D** | **D** | **C** |

              | **C** | **D** | **D** | **D** | **D**   ‖

Chorus 4

         G   **Bm**
I don't know where the sunbeams end
        C   **D**
And the star lights be - gin,
        G
It's all a mystery.
           Em   **D**
(Won't you stand up and be a man)
          G   **Bm**
And I don't know how a man decides
      C   **D**
What's right for his own life,
        G
It's all a mystery.
           Em   **D**
(When you're not prepared to face them.)
        G   **Bm**
I don't know where the sunbeams end
        C   **D**
And the star lights be - gin,
        G
It's all a mystery.
           Em   **D** | **D** |
(But in - stead I let him take you)
             G
It's all a myste - ry.
       N.C.
(The test is over. Now.)

Forget About Tomorrow

Words & Music by
Grant Nicholas

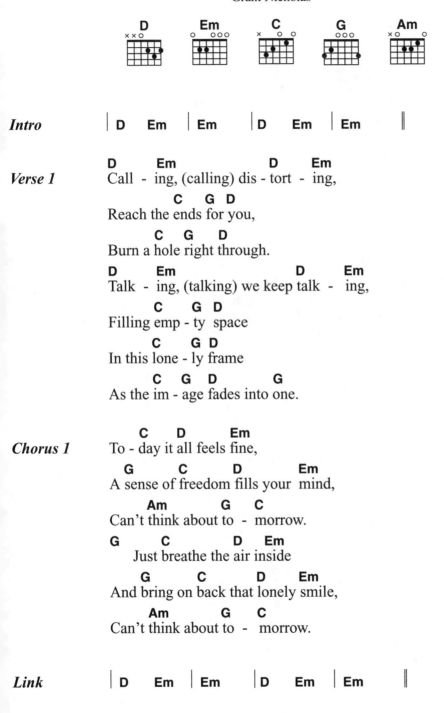

Intro |D Em |Em |D Em |Em   ‖

Verse 1

D   Em   D   Em
Call - ing, (calling) dis - tort - ing,

           C   G D
Reach the ends for you,

           C   G   D
Burn a hole right through.

D   Em   D   Em
Talk - ing, (talking) we keep talk - ing,

           C   G D
Filling emp - ty space

           C   G D
In this lone - ly frame

           C G D   G
As the im - age fades into one.

Chorus 1

            C   D   Em
To - day it all feels fine,

      G   C   D   Em
A sense of freedom fills your mind,

          Am   G   C
Can't think about to - morrow.

G   C   D   Em
      Just breathe the air inside

        G   C   D   Em
And bring on back that lonely smile,

          Am   G   C
Can't think about to - morrow.

Link |D Em |Em |D Em |Em   ‖

Verse 1

```
D      Em                   D      Em
Twist- ing (twisting), con - strict - ing,
              C   G D
On the edge for you,
                      C     G   D
You know I'd jump right through.
D        Em                 D      Em
Fall  -  ing (falling), we keep stall  -  ing,
              C  G D
I can see the ground,
                      C    G D
Some place near to land,
                  C     G   D         G
As the im  -  age fades into one.
```

Chorus 2

```
                  C    D    Em
To - day it all feels fine,
       G      C       D      Em
A sense of freedom fills your mind,
            Em       G    C
Can't think about to - morrow.
G       C          D   Em
    Just breathe the air inside,
          G        C       D      Em
And bring on back that lonely  smile,
            Am       G    C
Can't think about to - morrow,
            Am       G    C
Can't think about to - morrow,
```

Bridge

```
                  Em  C  G      D    Am         Em
Because you, feel your - self fall apart a - gain,
          C    G   D      Am         Em
You hold your face in - side your aching hands,
            C    G  D         Am            Em
The an - gels  tears come flooding down a - gain,
C     G D        | D  | D   | D    ‖
Bring us back again.
```

Link 2

```
      | D    Em  | Em     | D    Em   | Em        ‖
```

22

Verse 3

```
D     Em    D      Em
```
Yearn - ing, re - turn - ing,
```
        C    G D
```
To this emp - ty street
```
        C    G D
```
As the ci - ty sleeps.
```
D     Em            D      Em
```
Tear - ing, (tearing) des - pair - ing
```
        C   G     D
```
As the day comes in,
```
        C    G D
```
As the morn - ing sings
```
        C    G  D        G
```
As the im - age fades into one.

Chorus 3

```
        C    D     Em
```
To - day it all feels fine,
```
   G     C     D      Em
```
A sense of freedom fills your mind,
```
        Am        G   C
```
Can't think about to - morrow.
```
G      C           D   Em
```
   Just breathe the air inside,
```
   G      C         D   Em
```
And bring on back that lonely smile,
```
        Am        G   C
```
Can't think about to - morrow,
```
        C    D     Em
```
To - day it all feels fine,
```
   G     C     D       Em
```
A sense of freedom fills your mind,
```
        Am        G   C
```
Can't think about to - morrow.
```
G      C           D   Em
```
   Just breathe the air inside,
```
   G      C          D   Em
```
And bring on back that lonely smile,
```
        Am        G   C
```
Can't think about to - morrow,
```
        Am        G   C
```
Can't think about to - morrow.

For What It's Worth

Words & Music by
Peter Svensson & Nina Persson

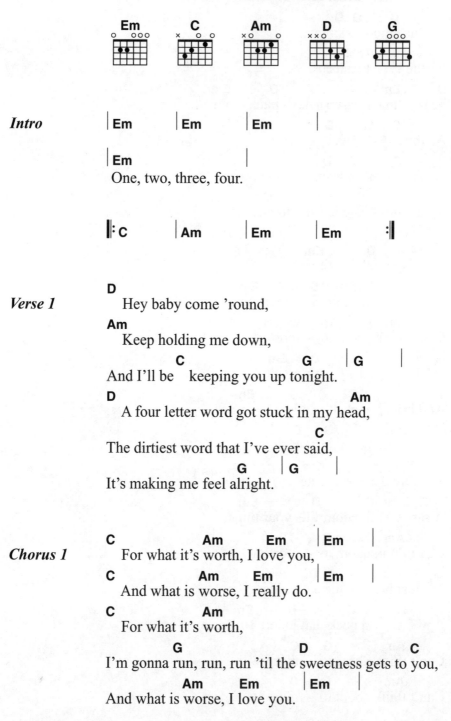

Intro | Em | Em | Em |

| Em |
One, two, three, four.

||: C | Am | Em | Em   :||

Verse 1
D
        Hey baby come 'round,
Am
        Keep holding me down,
                    C   G | G |
And I'll be   keeping you up tonight.
D   Am
        A four letter word got stuck in my head,
                                                    C
The dirtiest word that I've ever said,
                                    G | G |
It's making me feel alright.

Chorus 1
            C   Am   Em | Em |
        For what it's worth, I love you,
            C   Am   Em | Em |
        And what is worse, I really do.
            C   Am
        For what it's worth,
                        G   D   C
I'm gonna run, run, run 'til the sweetness gets to you,
                        Am   Em | Em |
And what is worse, I love you.

Verse 2

D
Hey please baby come back,
　　　　　Am
There'll be　 no more lovin' attacks,
　　　　　　C　　　　　　　　G　 |G　　　　|
And I'll be　 keeping it cool tonight.
D　　　　　　　　　　　　　Am
　The four letter word is out of my head,
　　　　　　　　　　　　　C
Come on around, get back in my bed,
　　　　　　　　　G　 |G　　　　|
Keep making me feel alright.

Chorus 2

C　　　　　　Am　　 Em　 |Em　　|
　For what it's worth, I like you,
C　　　　　　Am　　 Em　 |Em　　|
　And what is worse, I really do.
C　　　　　　　　Am
　Things have been worse,
　　　　　　　 G　　　　　D　　　 C
And we had fun, fun, fun 'til I said I love you,
　　　　　　 Am　　 Em　　　 |Em　　|
And what is worse, I really do.

Middle

C　　　　　　Am　　 Em　 |Em　　|
　For what it's worth, I love you,
C　　　　　　Am　　 Em
　And what is worse, I really do.

Interlude　 ‖: D　　|D　　 |Am　 |Am　 |C　　|C　　 |G　 |G　 :‖
Oh

Chorus 3

C　　　　　　Am　　 Em　 |Em　　|
　For what it's worth, I love you,
C　　　　　　Am　　 Em　 |Em　　|
　And what is worse, I really do, oh.
C　　　　　　Am　　 Em　 |Em　　|
　For what it's worth, I love you,
C　　　　　　Am　　 Em　 |Em　　|
　And what is worse, I really do.

Outro

               C
Oh, oh, oh, oh, oh, oh, oh.

Am   **Em**
  Oh, oh, oh, oh, oh, oh, oh.

               C
Oh, oh, oh, oh, oh, oh, oh.

Am   **Em**
  Oh, oh, oh, oh, oh, oh, oh.

               C   **Am**
Oh, oh, oh, oh, oh, oh, oh.

| **G** | **D** | **C** | **Am** | |

| **Em** | |

If You're Not The One

Words & Music by
Daniel Bedingfield

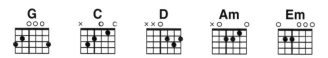

Verse 1

G
If you're not the one,

                                         C
Then why does my soul feel glad today?

G
If you're not the one,

                                       C
Then why does my hand fit yours this way?

G
If you are not mine,

                                    C
Then why does your heart return my call?

G
If you are not mine,

                                C
Would I have the strength to stand at all?

D   C
    I never know what the future brings,

               D   Am
But I know you're here with me now.

C   G
We'll make it through,

                                  C
And I hope you are the one I share my life with.

Chorus 1

G
    I don't wanna run away,

     Am   C   G
But I can't take it, I don't understand.

            Am
If I'm not made for you,

     C   Em
Then why does my heart tell me that I am?

          D   Am   C
Is there any way that I could stay in your arms?

Verse 2

```
       G
If I don't need you,
                        C
Then why am I crying on my bed?
    G
If I don't need you,
                             C
Then why does your name resound in my head?
    G
If you're not for me,
                           C
Then why does this distance maim my life?
    G
If you're not for me,
                          C
Then why do I dream of you as my wife?
D                        C
  I don't know why you're so far away,
     D                    Am
But I know that this much is true,
C          G
We'll make it through,
                              C
And I hope you are the one I share my life with.
G                              C
  And I wish that you could be the one I die with.
G                                C
  And I pray that you're the one I build my home with.
D       C              G
  I hope I love you all my life.
```

Chorus 2

```
        G
   I don't wanna run away,
   Am           C          G
But I can't take it, I don't understand.
            Am
If I'm not made for you,
       C                              Em
Then why does my heart tell me that I am?
            D              Am         C
Is there any way that I could stay in your arms?
```

28

Middle

      Em   **D**
'Cause I miss you, body and soul so strong,

            C
That it takes my breath away.

    Em
And I breathe you,

         D   **C**
Into my heart and pray for strength to stand today.

     Em
'Cause I love you,

          D
Whether it's wrong or right,

       G   **C**
And though I can't be with you tonight,

       D   **G**
You know my heart is by your side.

Chorus 3

   G
   I don't wanna run away,

  Am   **C**   **G**
But I can't take it, I don't understand.

     Am
If I'm not made for you,

    C   **Em**
Then why does my heart tell me that I am?

   D   **Am**   **C**
Is there any way that I could stay in your arms?

|**C** |**C**   ‖

In My Place

Words & Music by
Guy Berryman, Jon Buckland, Will Champion & Chris Martin

G	Bm	D	Em

Intro

‖ 2 bars drums ‖

‖: G | Bm D | G Em | Bm D :‖

Verse 1

G   Bm   D   G
  In my place, in my place were lines that I couldn't change
  Em Bm D
I was lost, oh yeah.
G   Bm   D   G
  I was lost, I was lost, crossed lines I shouldn't have crossed
  Em Bm D
I was lost, oh yeah.

Chorus 1

C   G   D C
Yeah, how long must you wait for it?
       G   D C
Yeah, how long must you pay for it?
       G   D C
Yeah, how long must you wait for it?
D
  Ah, for it?

Link

| G | Bm D | G Em | Bm D ‖

Verse 2

    G   Bm   D   G

I was scared, I was scared, tired and under-prepared,

       Em   Bm   D

But I'll wait for it.

    G   Bm   D   G

And if you go, if you go and leave me down here on my own,

      Em   Bm   D

Then I'll wait for you, yeah.

Chorus 2

C   G   D   C

Yeah, how long must you wait for it?

            G   D   C

Yeah, how long must you pay for it?

            G   D   C

Yeah, how long must you wait for it?

       D

Ah, for it?

Instrumental ‖: G | Bm   D | G   Em | Bm   D   :‖

Middle

          G   Bm

Singing: Please, please, please,

       D   G   Em   Bm

Come back and sing to me, to me, ah me.

       D   G   Bm

Come on and sing it out, now, now

       D   G   Em Bm

Come on and sing it out, to me, me

       D

Come back and sing it.

Outro

    G   Bm   D   G

In my place, in my place were lines that I couldn't change

      Em   D

I was lost, oh yeah.

    D G

Oh yeah.

I'm Gonna Getcha Good!

Words & Music by
Shania Twain & Robert John "Mutt" Lange

Em	D	G	C	Am

Intro |Em |G D |Em |G D |

Verse 1

          Em N.C.   G   D
Don't want ya for the weekend,

          Em N.C.   Em D
Don't want ya for a night.

      N.C.   G   D   Em   D
I'm only interested if I can have you for life,   yeah.

      Em   G   D
I know I sound serious,

      Em   G   D
And baby I am

          Em
You're a fine piece of real estate,

    G   D   Em
And I'm gonna get me some land.

G   D
   Oh, yeah.

Bridge 1

    D   C
   So, don't try to run honey,

    D   C
   Love can be fun.

    G   Am
   There's no need to be alone,

            C
When you find that someone.

Chorus 1

    G   D
   I'm gonna getcha while I gotcha in sight,

Em   C
   I'm gonna getcha if it takes all night,

G   D
   You can betcha by the time I say go,

        C
You'll never say no.

  G   **D**
  I'm gonna getcha, it's a matter of fact

Em   **C**
  I'm gonna getcha, don't ya worry 'bout that

G   **D**
  You can bet your bottom dollar

          C
In time you're gonna be mine.

        D   **Em** | **G** **D** |
Just like I should, I'll getcha good,   yeah.

| **Em** | **G** **D** |

Em   **G**   **D**
Verse 2   I've already planned it,

      Em   **G**   **D**
Here's how it's gonna be,

      Em
I'm gonna love you,

      G   **D**   **Em**
And you're gonna fall in love with me.

      G   **D**
Yeah, yeah.

Bridge 2   As Bridge 1

  G   **D**
Chorus 2   I'm gonna getcha while I gotcha in sight,

Em   **C**
  I'm gonna getcha if it takes all night,

G   **D**
  You can betcha by the time I say go,

      C
You'll never say no.

G   **D**
  I'm gonna getcha, it's a matter of fact

Em   **C**
  I'm gonna getcha, don't ya worry 'bout that

G   **D**
  You can bet your bottom dollar

       C
In time you're gonna be mine.

      D   **Em** | **G** **D** | **Em** | **G** **D** |
Just like I should, I'll getcha good.

                                    Em
Middle   Yeah, I'm gonna getcha baby,

                  I'm gonna knock on wood.

                  I'm gonna getcha somehow honey yeah,

                  I'm gonna make it good.

                  Yeah, yeah, yeah, yeah.

                  Oh, yeah.

Bridge 3   As Bridge 1

                  G   **D**
Chorus 3   I'm gonna getcha while I gotcha in sight,
                  Em   **C**
                     I'm gonna getcha if it takes all night,
                  G   **D**
                     You can betcha by the time I say go,
                          C
                  You'll never say no.
                  G   **D**
                     I'm gonna getcha, it's a matter of fact
                  Em   **C**
                     I'm gonna getcha, don't ya worry 'bout that
                  G   **D**
                     You can bet your bottom dollar
                              C
                  In time you're gonna be mine.

                                      G
Outro   Oh, I'm gonna getcha,
                  D   **Em** **C**
                     I'm gonna getcha real good.
                                    G
                  Yeah, you can betcha,
                  D   **C**
                     Oh, I'm gonna getcha.
                              D   **Em**
                  Just like I should, I'll getcha good,

                  Oh, I'm gonna getcha good.

                  | **Em**   ‖

Just Like A Pill

Words & Music by
Dallas Austin & Alecia Moore

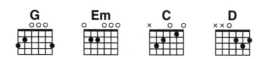

Intro | G | Em | C | D ‖

Verse 1

G   Em   C
    I'm lying here on the floor where you left me,
D
I think I took too much.
G   Em   C
    I'm crying here, what have you done?
D
I thought it would be fun.

Bridge 1

C   D
    I can't stay on your life support,
                           C
There's a shortage in the switch.
                     D
I can't stay on your morphine,
                     C
'Cause it's making me itch.
                     D
I said I tried to call the nurse again,
                     C
But she's being a little bitch.
                    D
I'll think I'll get out of here,

	G Em
Chorus 1	Where I can run just as fast as I can,

                                    C
              To the middle of no - where,

                                    D
              To the middle of my frustrated fears,

                 G   Em
              And I swear, you're just like a pill,

                                    C
              Instead of making me better,

                                    D
              You keep making me ill,

                                    G | Em | C | D |
              You keep making me ill.

              G   Em   C
Verse 2   I haven't moved from the spot where you left me,

              D
                 It must be a bad trip.

              G   Em   C
                 All of the other pills they were different,

              D
              Maybe I should get some help.

Bridge 2   As Bridge 1

36

Chorus 2

                G   Em
Where I can run just as fast as I can,

                           C
To the middle of no - where,

                           D
To the middle of my frustrated fears.

                G   Em
And I swear, you're just like a pill,

                           C
Instead of making me better,

                           D
You keep making me ill,

You keep making me,
G   Em
Run just as fast as I can,

                           C
To the middle of no - where,

                           D
To the middle of my frustrated fears.

                G   Em
And I swear, you're just like a pill,

                           C
Instead of making me better,

                           D
You keep making me ill,

                           G
You keep making me ill.

Bridge 3   As Bridge 1

Chorus 3   As Chorus 2

Repeat Chorus to fade

Just A Little

Words & Music by
Michelle Escoffery, George Hammond Hagan & John Hammond Hagan

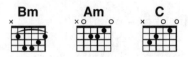

Intro | Bm | Bm | Bm | Bm ‖

Verse 1

Bm
Sexy, everything about you's so sexy,

        Am
You don't even know what you got,

      Bm
You're really hitting my spot, oh yeah.

And you're so innocent,

Please don't take this wrong 'cause it's a compliment,

        Am
I just wanna get with your flow,

     Bm
You gotta learn to let go,

Oh baby won't you,

Chorus 1

Bm
Work it a little, get hot just a little,

Meet me in the middle, let go,

    Am
Just a little bit more,

      Bm
Give me just a little bit more.

(Just a little bit more, just a little.)

Verse 2

Bm
Let me, I'll do anything if you'll just let me,

Am
Find a way to make you ex - plore,

Bm
I know you wanna break down those   walls, yeah, yeah.

And it's so challenging, getting close to you's what I'm imagining,

Am
I just wanna see you get   down,

Bm
You gotta let it all out,

Oh baby won't you just,

Chorus 2   As Chorus 1

Chorus 3   As Chorus 1

Middle

C   **Bm**
  It's so exciting, the way you're in - viting me.

(I like it when you do it like that ah,)

C   **Bm**   **Am**
  Can't get enough, won't you satis - fy my needs,

Chorus 4   As Chorus 1

Chorus 5   As Chorus 1

Chorus 6   As Chorus 1

Outro

Bm
Sexy, everything about you's so sexy

Am
You don't even know…

To fade

Love At First Sight

Words & Music by
Kylie Minogue, Richard Stannard, Julian Gallagher, Ash Howes & Martin Harrington

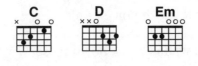

Intro | C | C | C | C |: C | D Em :‖ *x4*

Verse 1
C   D   Em
Thought that I was going crazy,
C   D   Em
Just having one those days yeah.
C   D   Em
Didn't know what to do,
C   D   Em
Then there was you.____

Bridge 1
      C   D   Em
And everything went from wrong to right,
              C   D   Em
And the stars came out and filled up the sky,
              C   D   Em
The music you were playing really blew my mind,
              C   D   Em
It was love, at first sight.

Chorus 1
             C   D   Em
'Cause baby when   I heard you,
C   D   Em
For the first   time I knew,
C   D   Em C | D   Em |
We were meant   to be as one._____

Interlude 1 | C | D Em | D Em | D Em |

	C	D	Em
Verse 2	Was tired of running out of luck,		

```
        C                 D      Em
        Was tired of running out of luck,
        C               D      Em
        Thinking 'bout giving up yeah,
        C           D      Em
        Didn't know what to do
        C               D      Em
        Then there was you.
```

Bridge 2   As Bridge 1

Chorus 2   As Chorus 1

Chorus 3   As Chorus 1

Interlude 2

```
                              x4
         ‖: C        | D    Em    :‖
```

Middle

```
            C                      D      Em
        And everything went from wrong to right,
              C                    D      Em
        And the stars came out and filled up the sky.
            C                        D      Em
        The music you were playing really blew my mind,
              C    D   Em
        It was love at first sight.
            C    D   Em
        Love at first sight,
            C    D   Em
        Love at first sight,
            C  D  Em         C
        Love,    oh it was love,
                   D    Em
        It was love at first sight.
```

Chorus 4   As Chorus 1

Chorus 5   As Chorus 1

Outro

```
            C
       ‖: It was love, it was love,
            D         Em
       It was love, it was love. :‖
```

Repeat to fade

Songbird

Words & Music by
Liam Gallagher

Intro

Spoken: Three four.

| G | G ‖

Verse 1

G
   Talking to the songbird yesterday
                          Em
Flew me to a place not far a - way.

She's a little pilot in my mind,
                    Em   G
Singing songs of love to pass the time.

Chorus 1

G
   Gonna write a song so she can see,
                    G   Em
Give her all the love she gives to me.

Talk of better days that have yet to come
                  Em   G
Never felt this love from anyone.___

She's not any - one,
         G   Em
She's not anyone.___
             Em
She's not anyone.

Verse 2

G
A man can never dream these kind of things

                                   G   Em
Especially when she came and spread her wings.

Whispered in my ear the things I'd like

                    Em G
Then she flew away in - to the night.

Chorus 2

Gonna write a song so she can see,

                      G   Em
Give her all the love she gives to me.

Talk of better days that have yet to come

                    Em   G
Never felt this love from anyone.

She's not anyone,

             G   Em
She's not any - one.____

She's not anyone.

Instrumental

G	G	G	G	G	
Em	Em	Em	Em	Em	
G	G	G	G	G	
Em	Em	Em	Em	Em	G

Wherever You Will Go

Words & Music by
Aaron Kamin & Alex Band

G   D   Em   C   Bm

Intro
```
| G    | D    | Em    | C    ||
```

Verse 1

```
      G           D
```
So lately, I've been wonderin'
```
Em          C              G
```
Who will be there to take my place
```
                   D
```
When I'm gone,   you'll need love
```
Em          C              G
```
To light the shadows on your face
```
      D              Em
```
If a great wave shall fall
```
      C          G
```
It'll fall upon us all
```
      D                    Em
```
And between the sand and stone
```
                C              G
```
Could you make it on your own.

Chorus 1

```
      G           D
```
If I could, then I would
```
Em          C              G
```
I'll go wherever you will go
```
              D
```
Way up high or down low
```
Em          C              G
```
I'll go wherever you will go.

Verse 2

```
      G           D
```
And maybe, I'll find out
```
Em          C                  G
```
A way to make it back some day

cont.

               D
To watch you, to guide you
Em   **C**   **G**
   Through the darkest of your days
     D   **Em**
If a great wave shall fall
     C   **G**
It'll fall upon us all
      D   **Em**
Well I hope there's someone out there
        C   **G**
Who can bring me back to you.

Chorus 2   As Chorus 1

Bridge
     C   **D**
Run away with my heart
     Bm   **Em**
Run away with my hope
     C   **D**   **Bm**
Run away with my love.

Verse 3
     G   **D**
   I know now,   just quite how
Em   **C**   **G**
   My life and love might still go on
              D
In your heart,   in your mind
Em   **C**
   I'll stay with you for all of time.

Chorus 3   As Chorus 1

Chorus 4
     G   **D**
   If I could turn back time
     Em   **C**
   I'll go wherever you will go
     G   **D**
   If I could make you mine
     Em   **C**
   I'll go wherever you will (go).

Outro   ‖: **G** |**D** |**Em** |**C**   :‖
              go.

Whenever, Wherever

Words by Shakira & Gloria Estefan
Music by Shakira & Tim Mitchell

Em   Am   D   Bm   C   G

Capo second fret

Intro ‖: Em | Em | Am | D :‖

Verse 1

Em
Lucky you were born that far away so
Bm
We could both make fun of distance.
C
Lucky that I love a foreign land for
G   D
The lucky fact of your existence.
Em
Baby I would climb the Andes solely
Bm
To count the freckles on your body.
C
Never could imagine there were only
G   D
Ten million ways to love somebody.

Bridge 1

Am
Le, do, le, le, le, le,
Em
Le, do, le, le, le, le.
C
Can't you see,
D
I'm at your feet.

Chorus 1

Em   C
Whenever,   wherever,
G   D
We're meant to be together,
Em   C
I'll be there and you'll be near,

	Am	D
cont.	And that's the deal my dear.

Am　　　　　**D**
And that's the deal my dear.

Em　　　**C**
There over,　here under,

G　　　　　**D**
You'll never have to wonder,

Em　　　　**C**
We can always play by ear,

Am　　　　　　**D**
But that's the deal my dear.

Interlude 1　| Em　　| Em　　| Am　　| D　　　　|

　　　　　　| Em　　| Em　　| Am　　| D　　| N.C.　| N.C.　　|

Verse 2

Em
Lucky that my lips not only mumble,

Bm
They spill kisses like a fountain.

C
Lucky that my breasts are small and humble,

G　　　　　　　　　**D**
So you don't confuse them　with mountains.

Em
Lucky I have strong legs like my mother,

Bm
To run for cover when I needed.

C
And these two eyes that for no other,

G　　　　　　　　　**D**
The day you leave will cry a river.

Bridge 2

Am
Le, do, le, le, le, le,

Em
Le, do, le, le, le, le.

C
At your feet,

D
I'm at your feet.

Chorus 2　　As Chorus 1

Interlude 2 | Em | Em | Am | D | Em | Em | N.C. | N.C. |

Middle
```
Am
Le, do, le, le, le, le,
Em
Le, do, le, le, le, le.
C
Think out loud,
D
Say it again.
Am
Le, do, le, le, le, le,
Em
Tell me one more time,
C
That you'll live,
D              | N.C. | N.C. |
Lost in my eyes.
```

Chorus 3
```
Em        C
Whenever,   wherever,
G              D
   We're meant to be together,
Em          C
I'll be there and you'll be near,
Am             D
   And that's the deal my dear.
Em        C
   There-over,   here-under,
G            D
You've got me head over heels,
Em          C
   There's nothing left to fear,
Am                  D
   If you really feel the way I feel.
```

Chorus 4   As Chorus 3

Outro | Em | Em | Am | Am |

| Em | Em | N.C. | N.C. |

48

2/05 (53934)